This Coloring Book Belongs To:

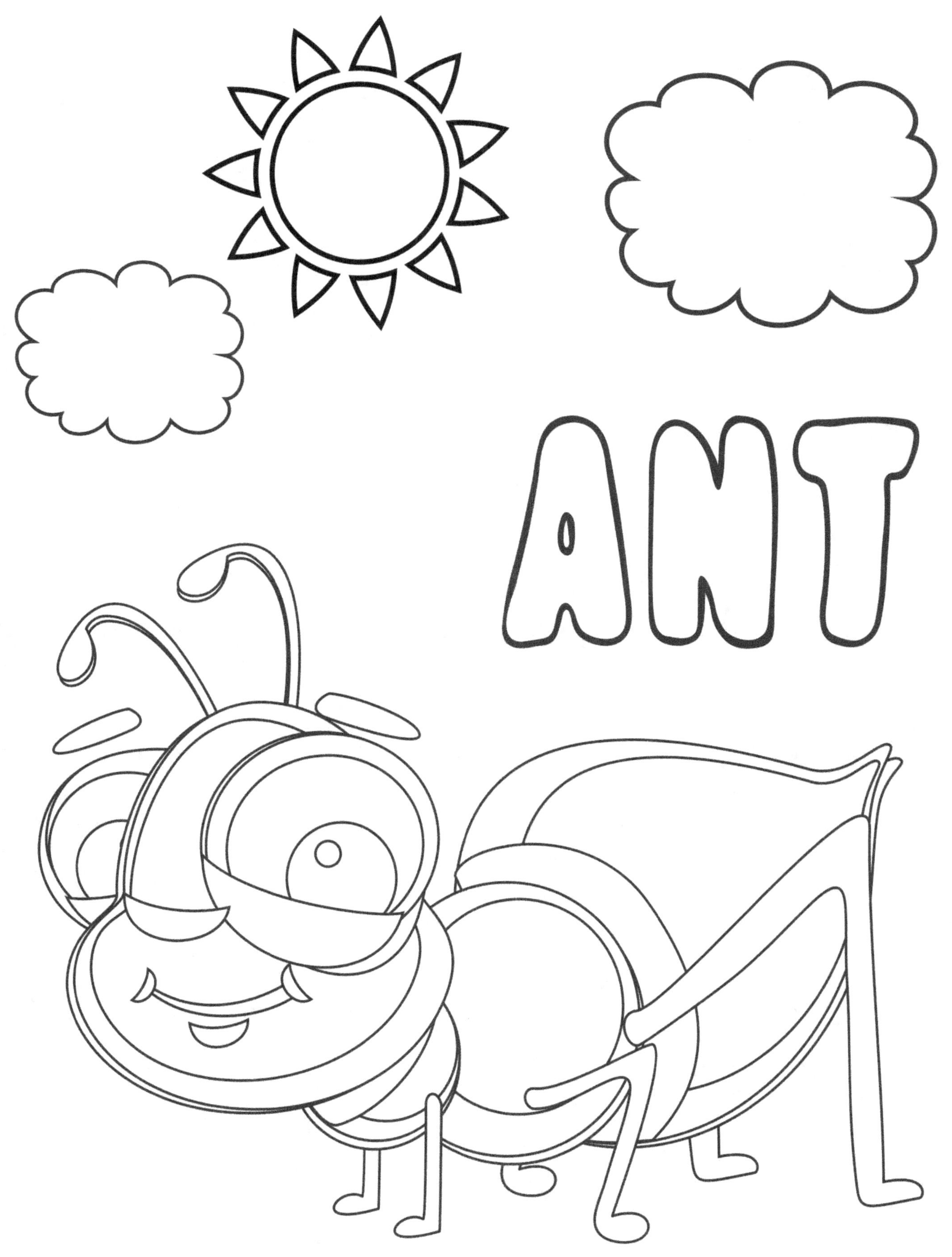

ANT

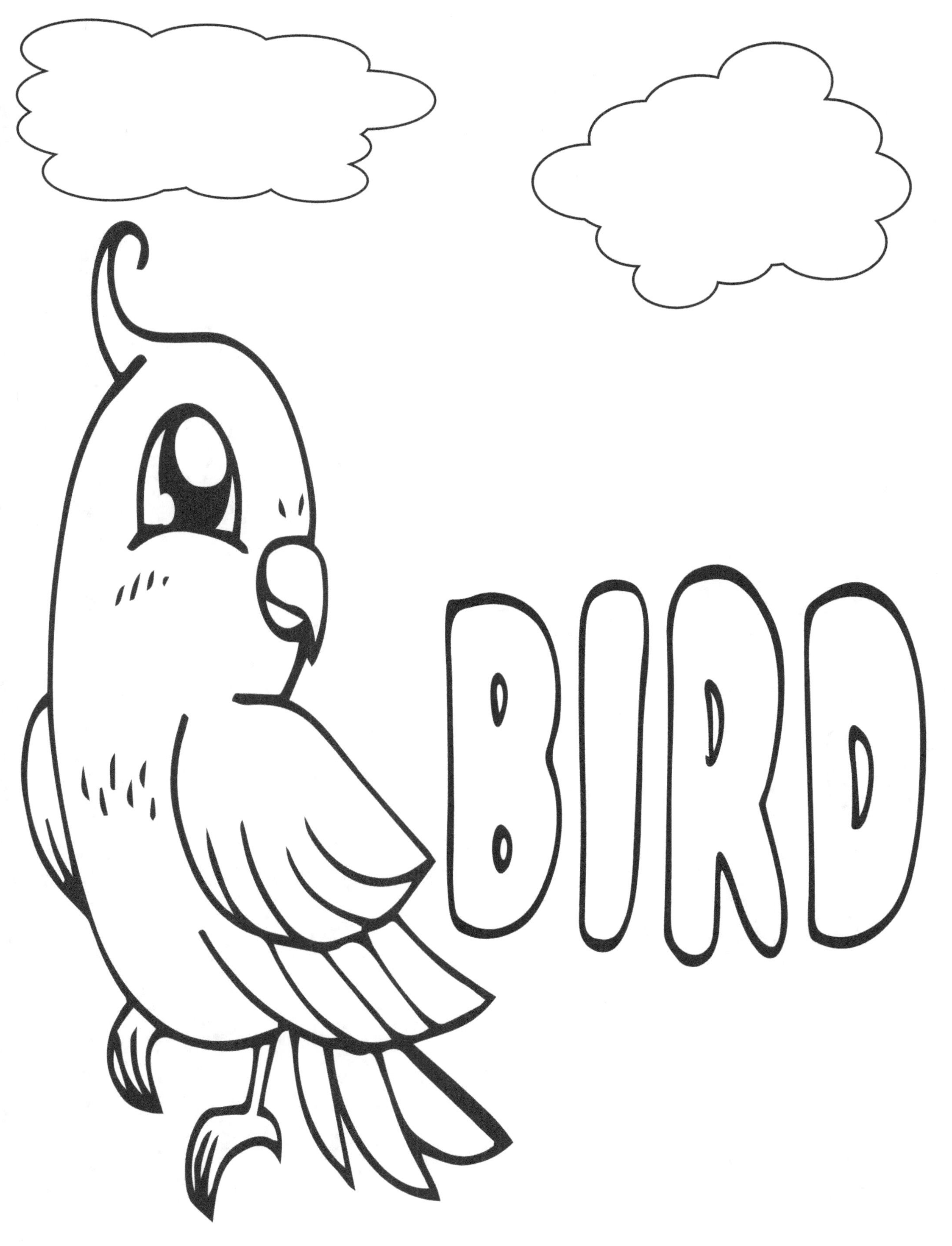
BIRD

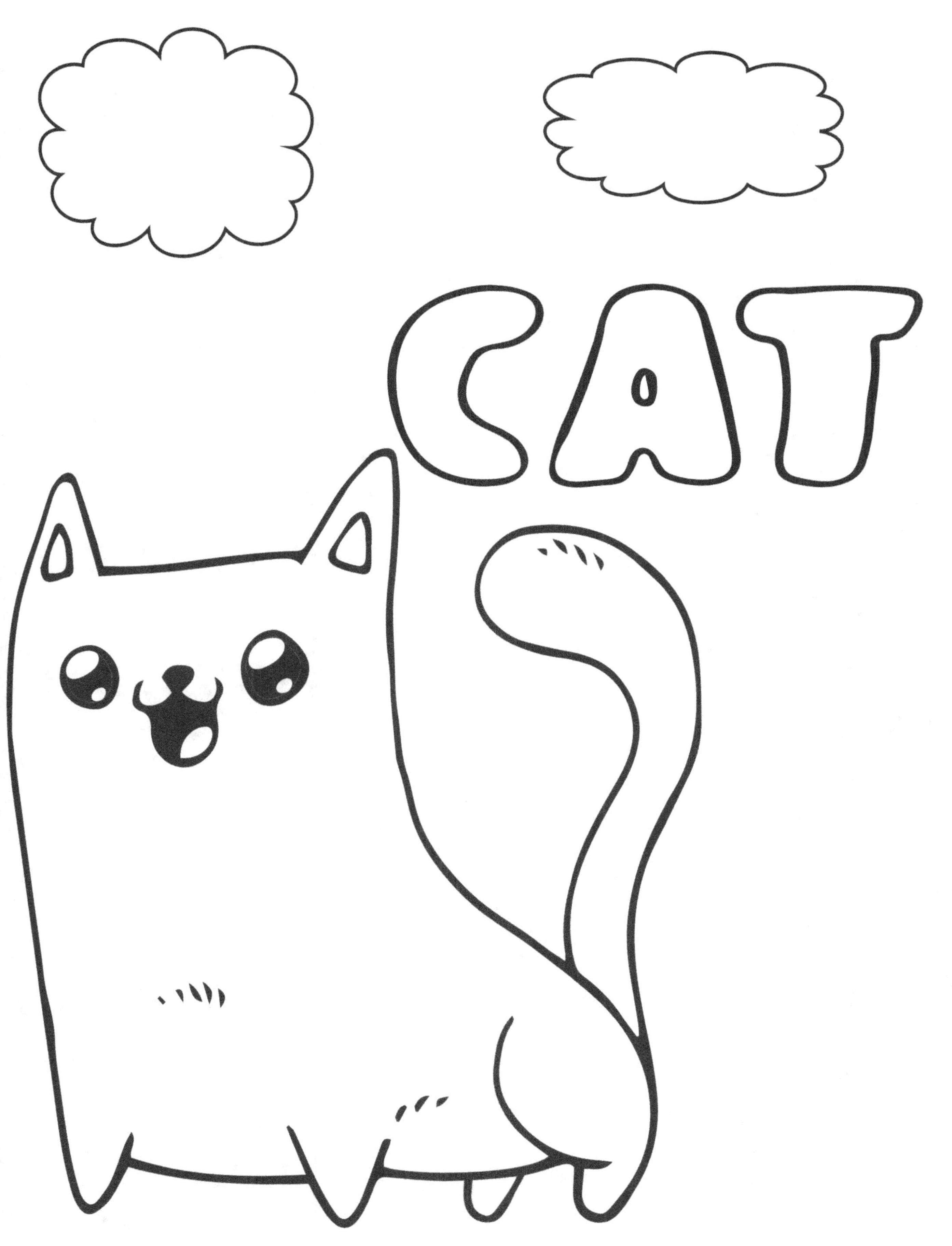

CAT

DEER

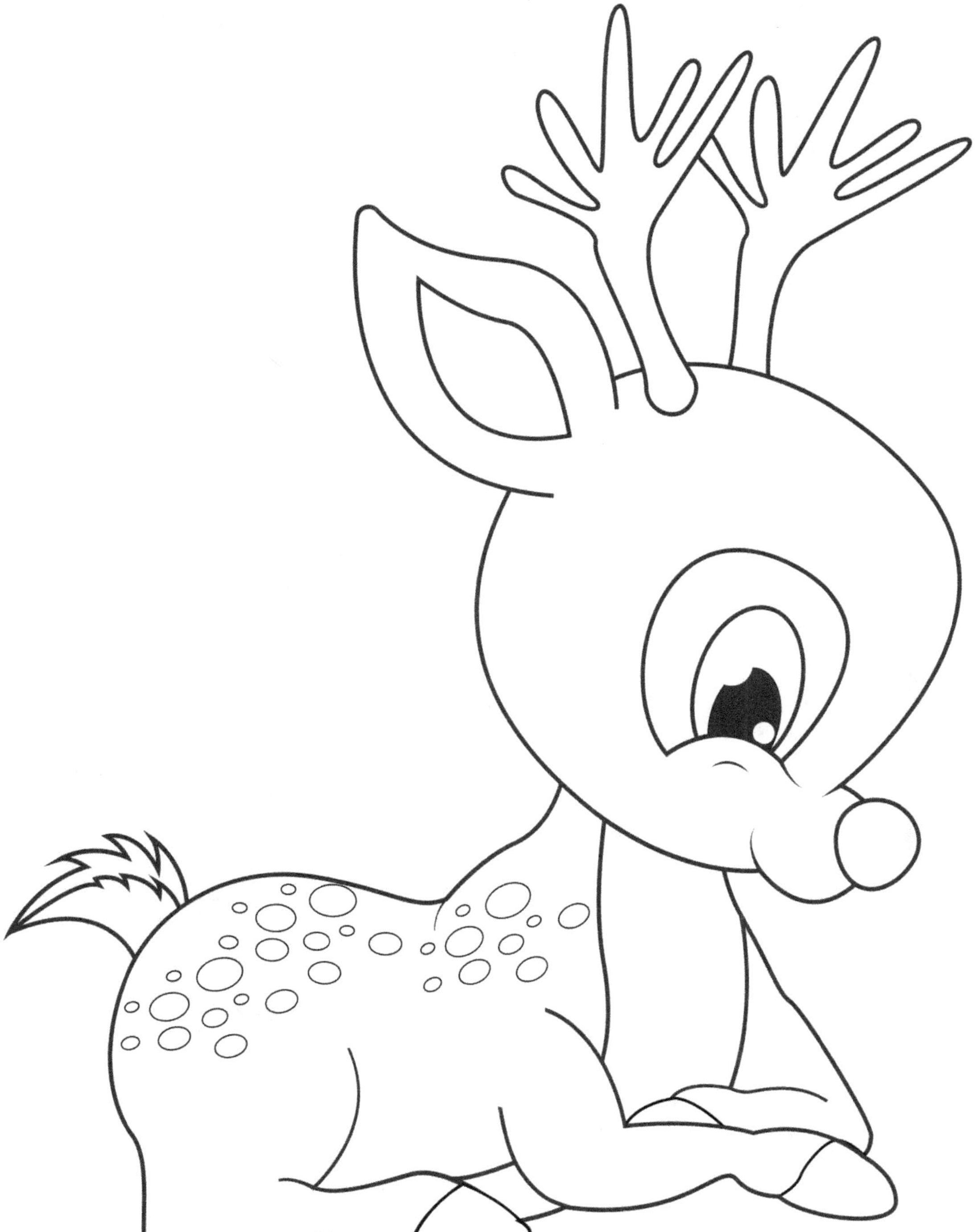

ELEPHANT

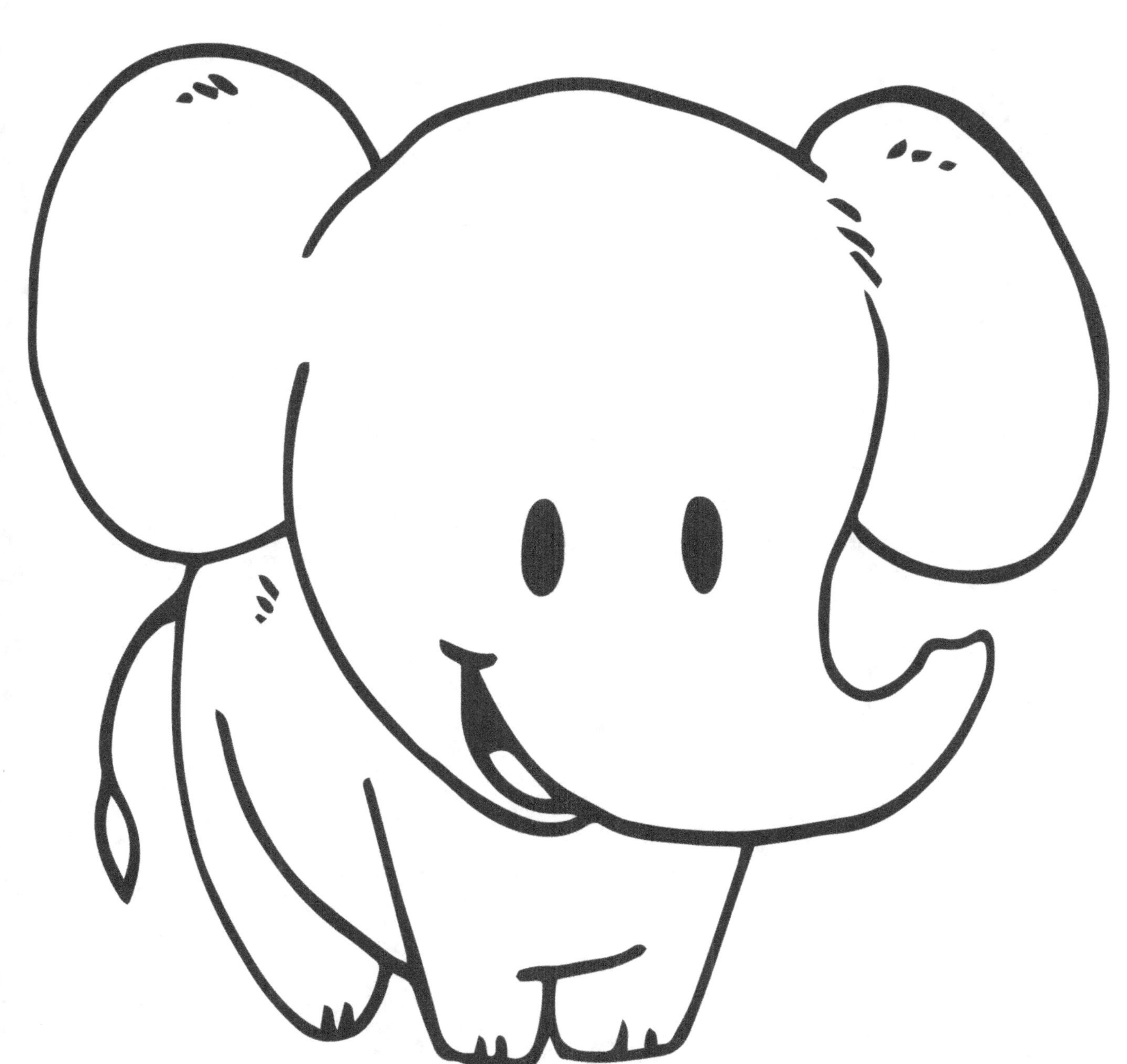

FROG

GIAFFE

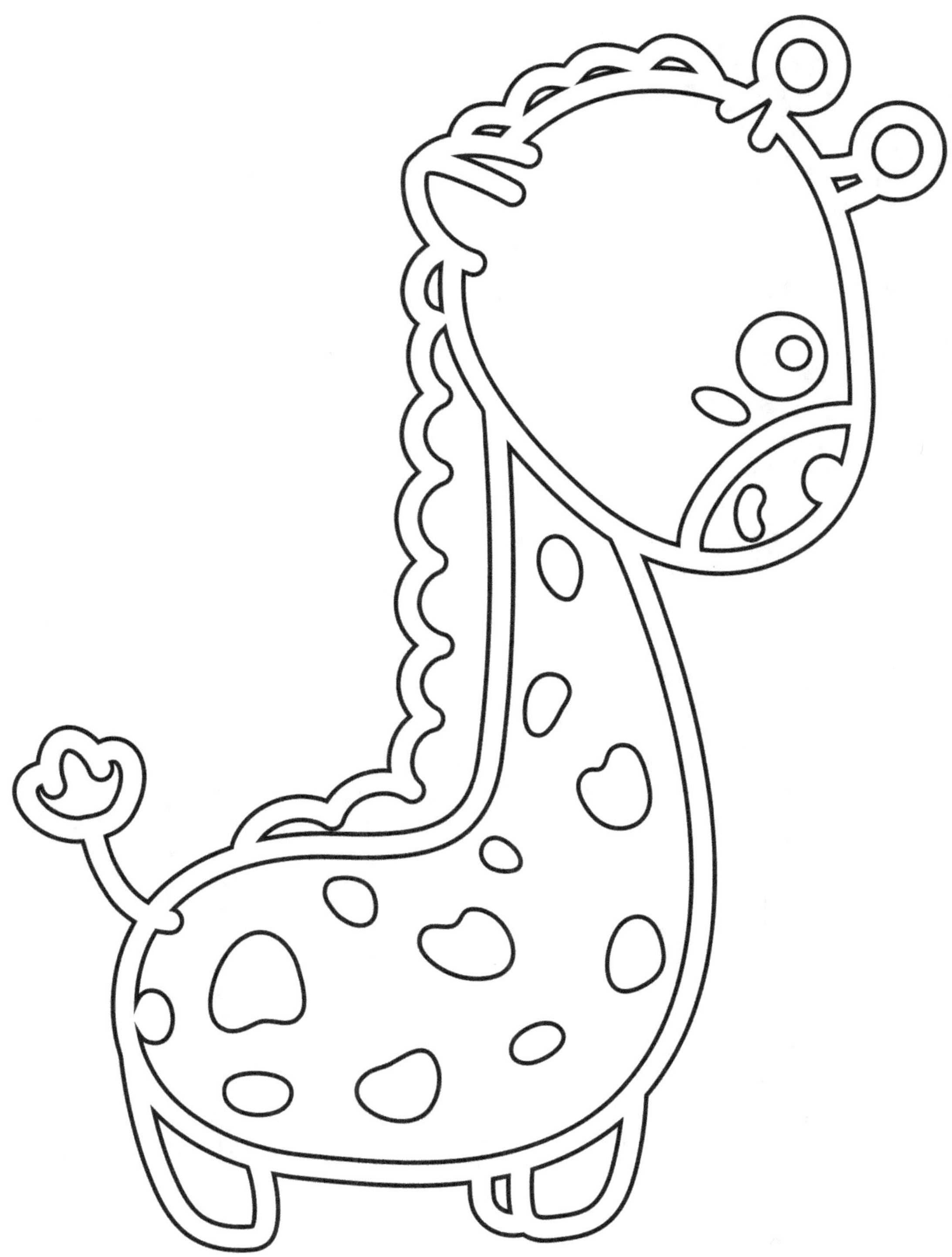

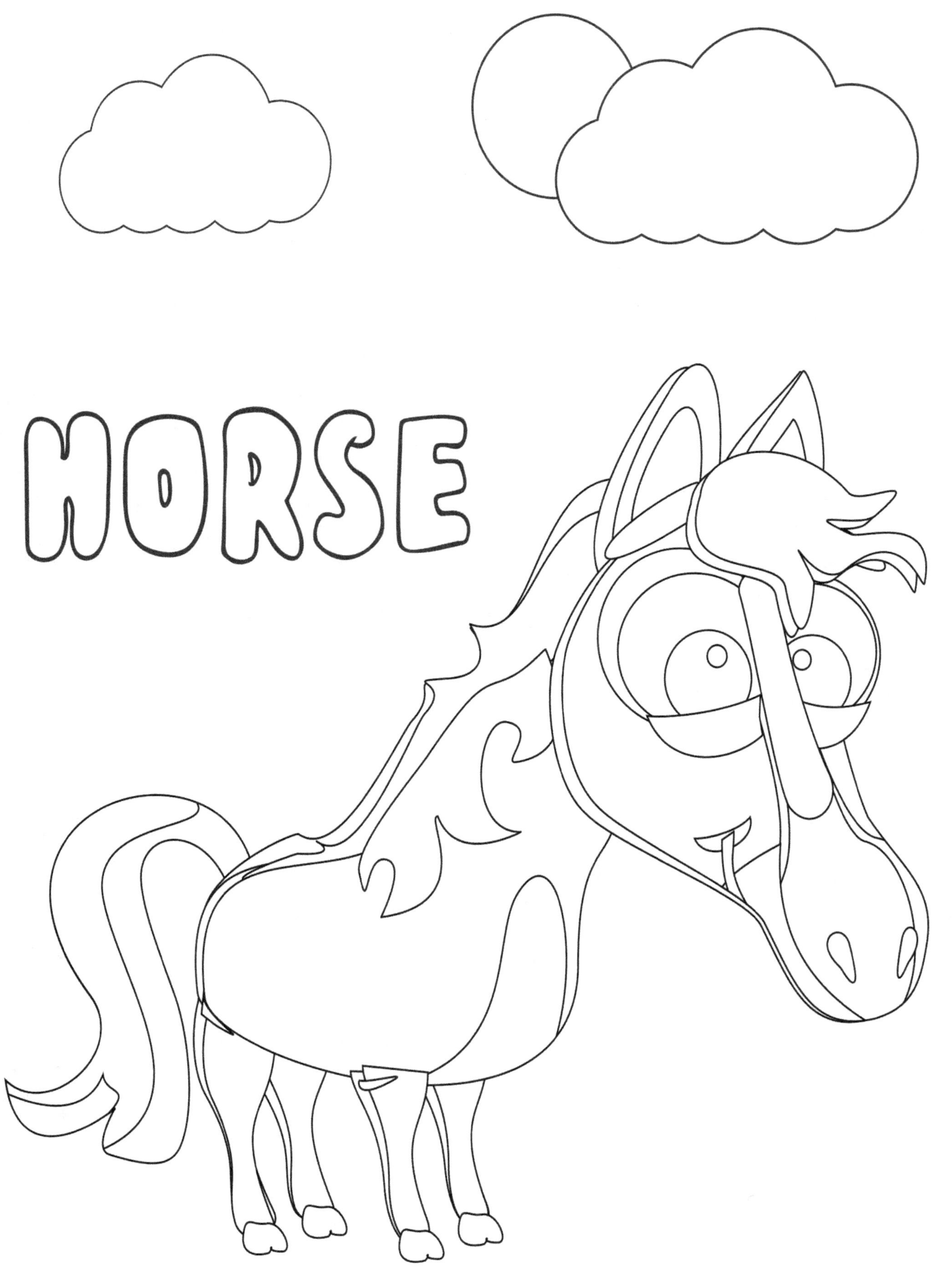

HORSE

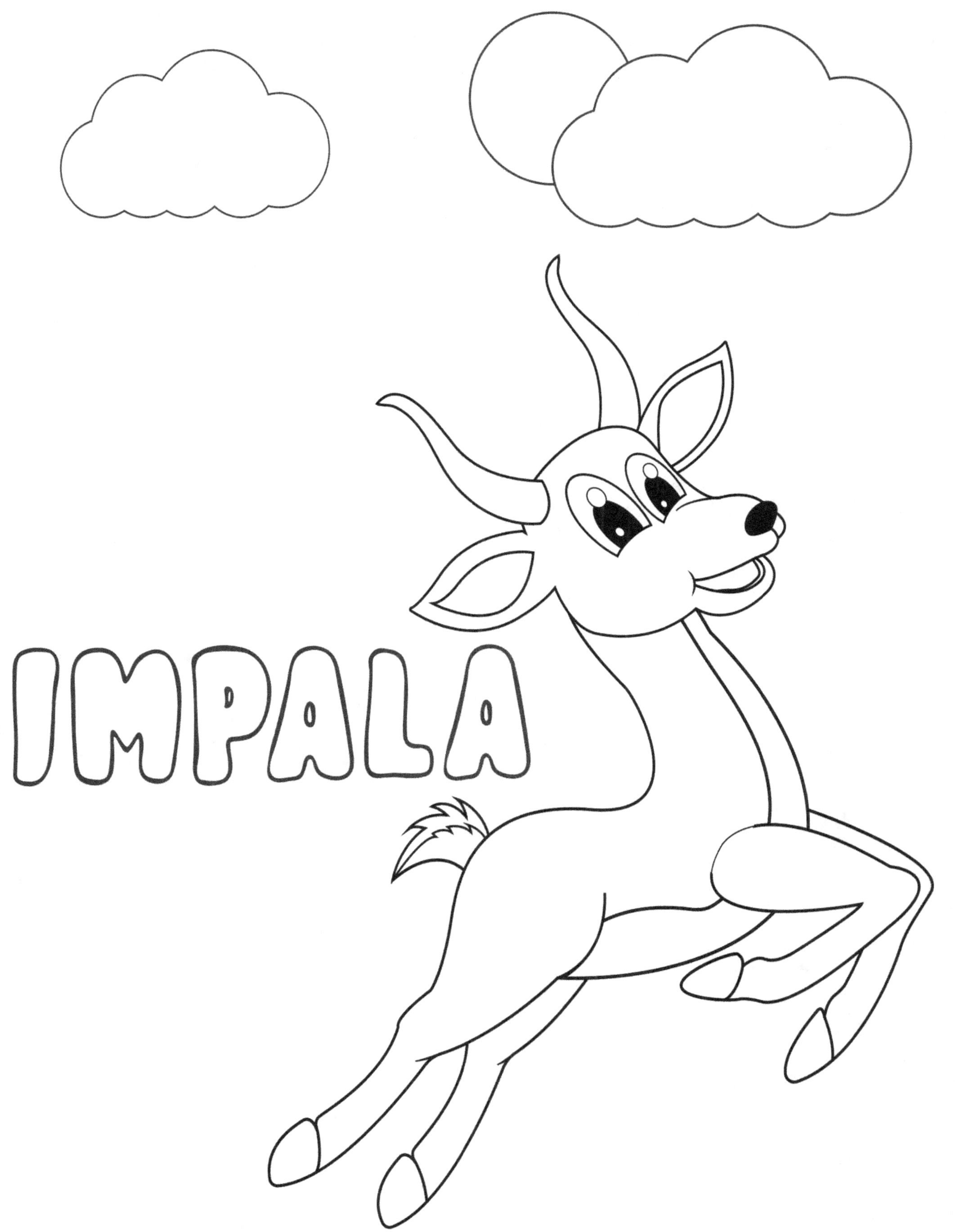

IMPALA

JAGUAR

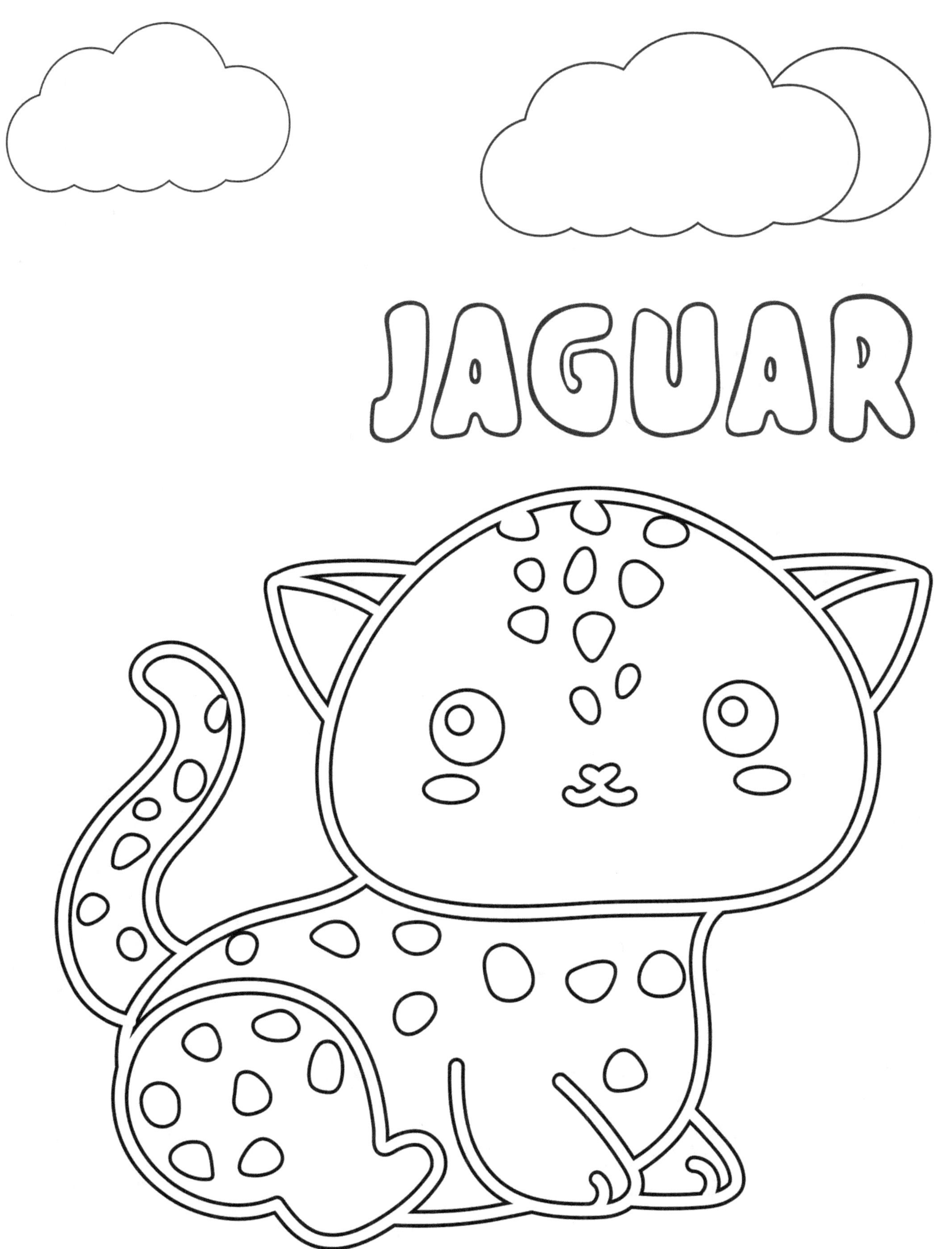

KANGAROO

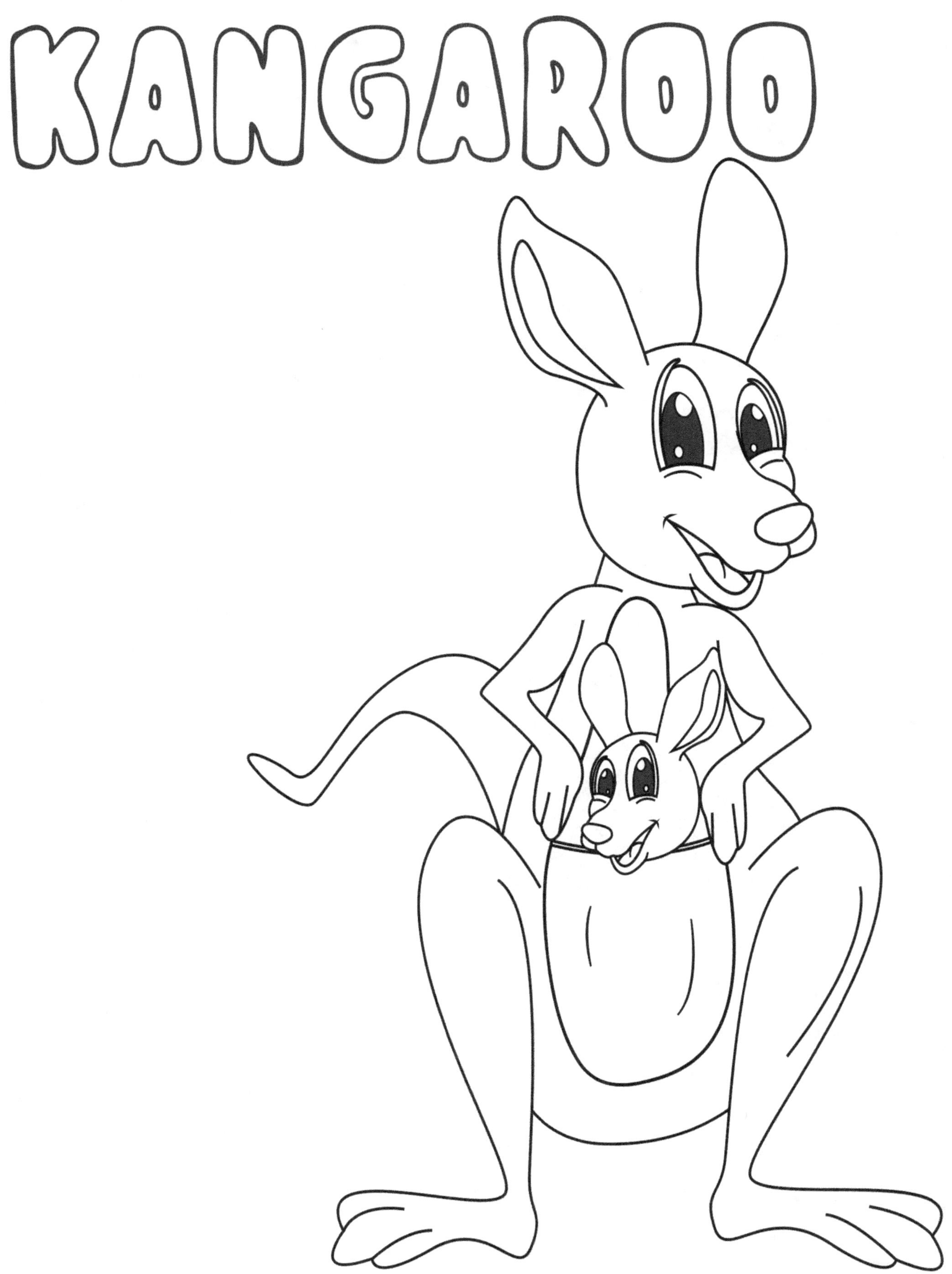

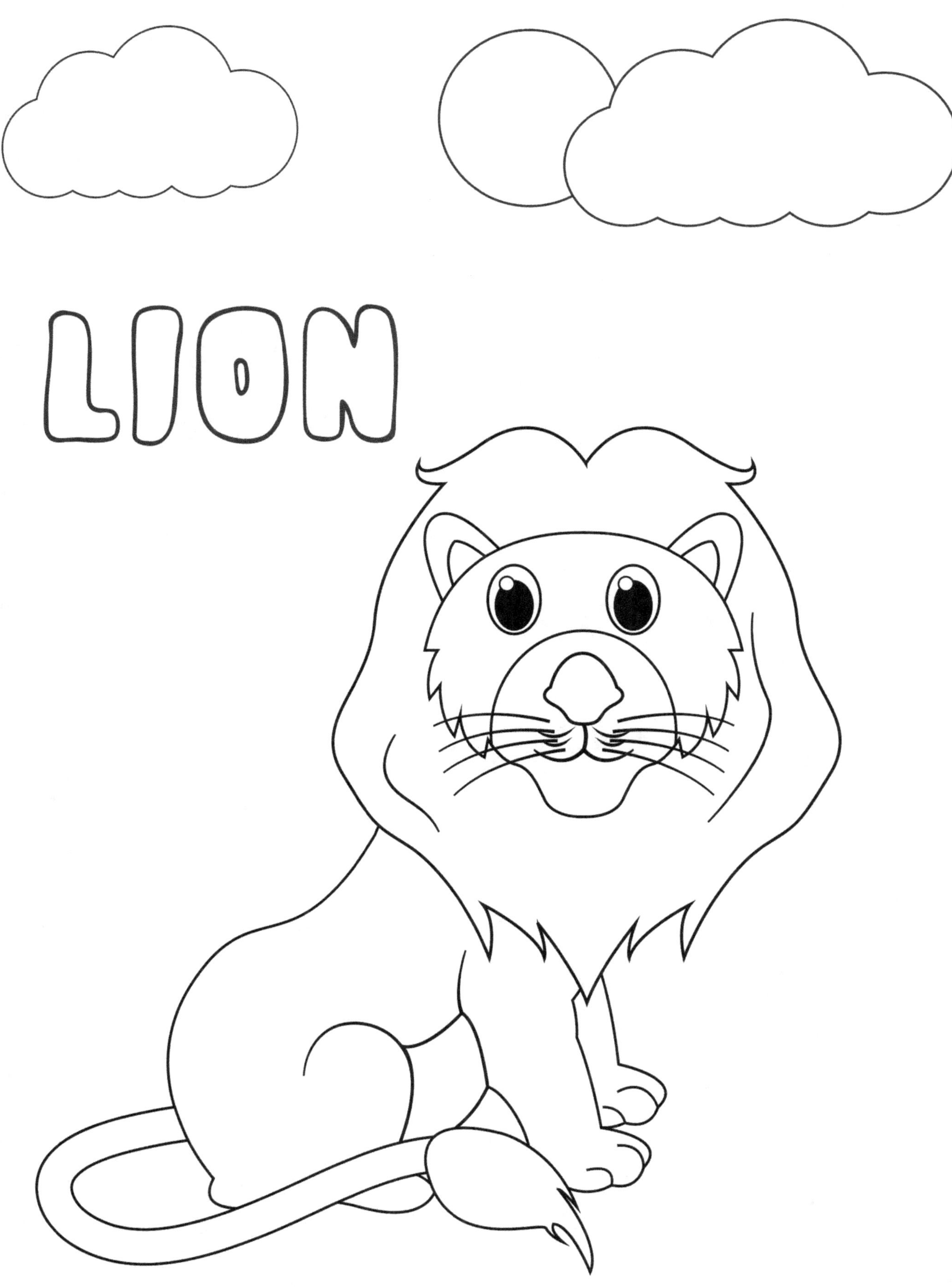

LION

MONKEY

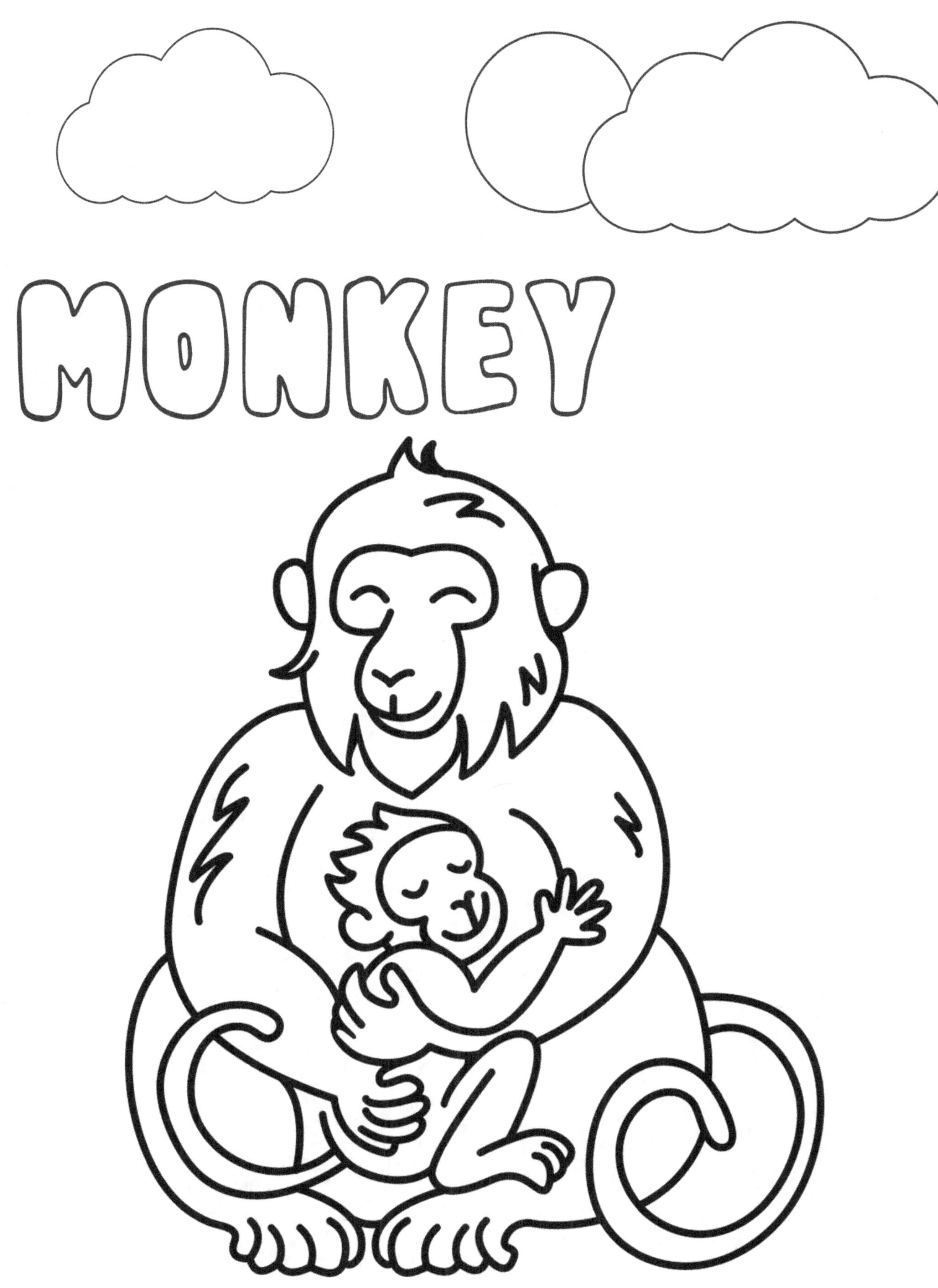

NUMBAT

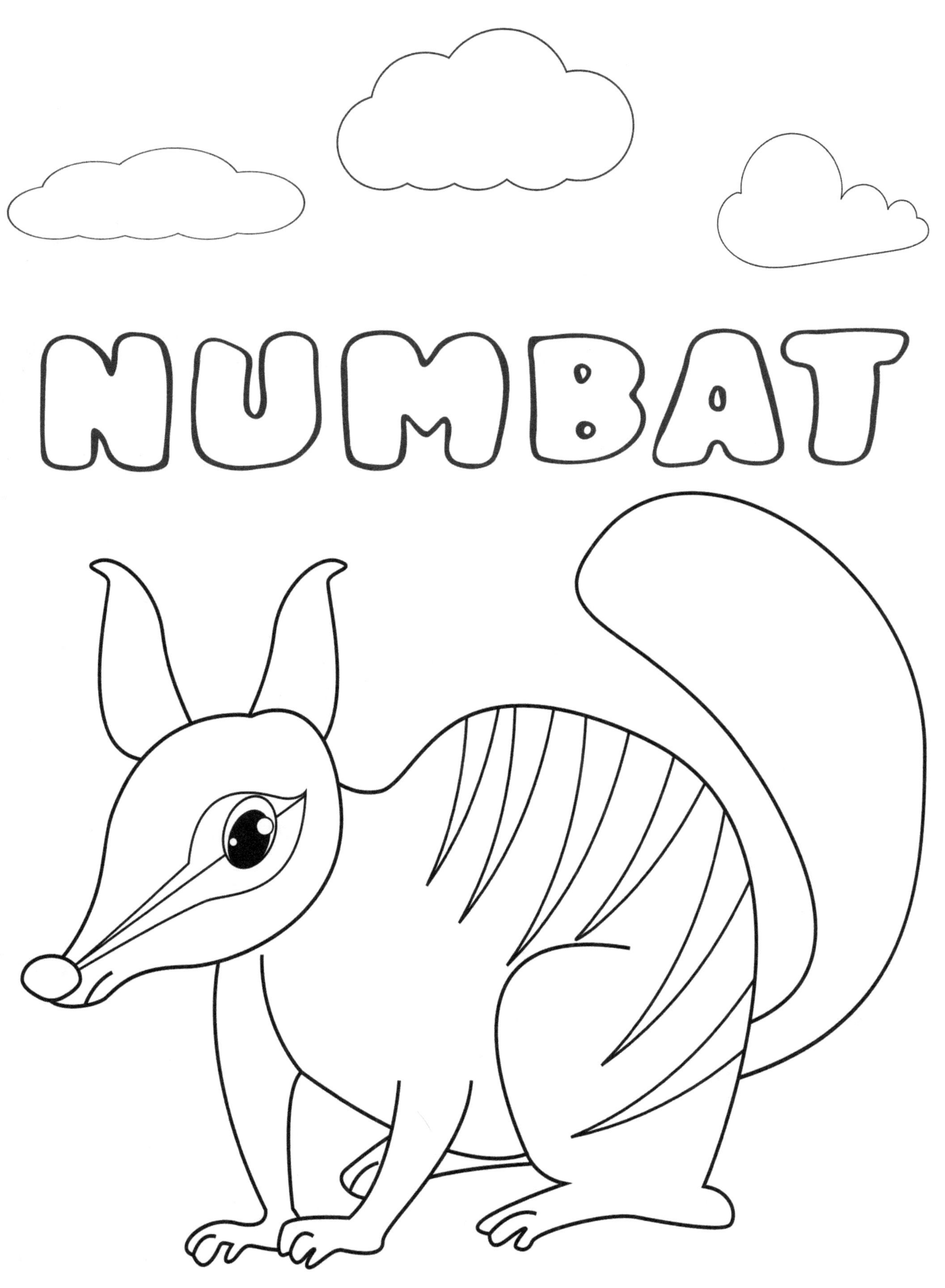

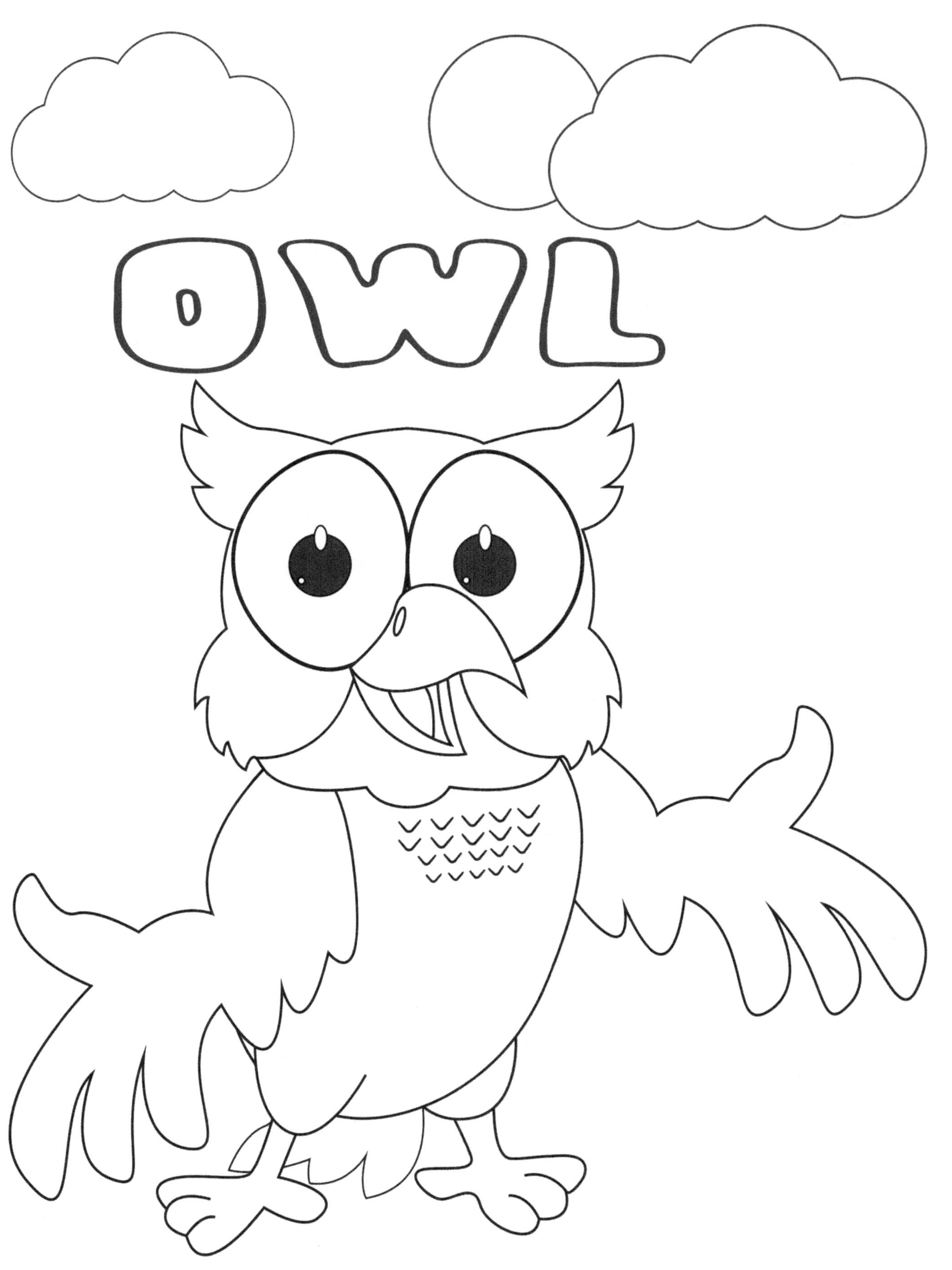
OWL

PANDA

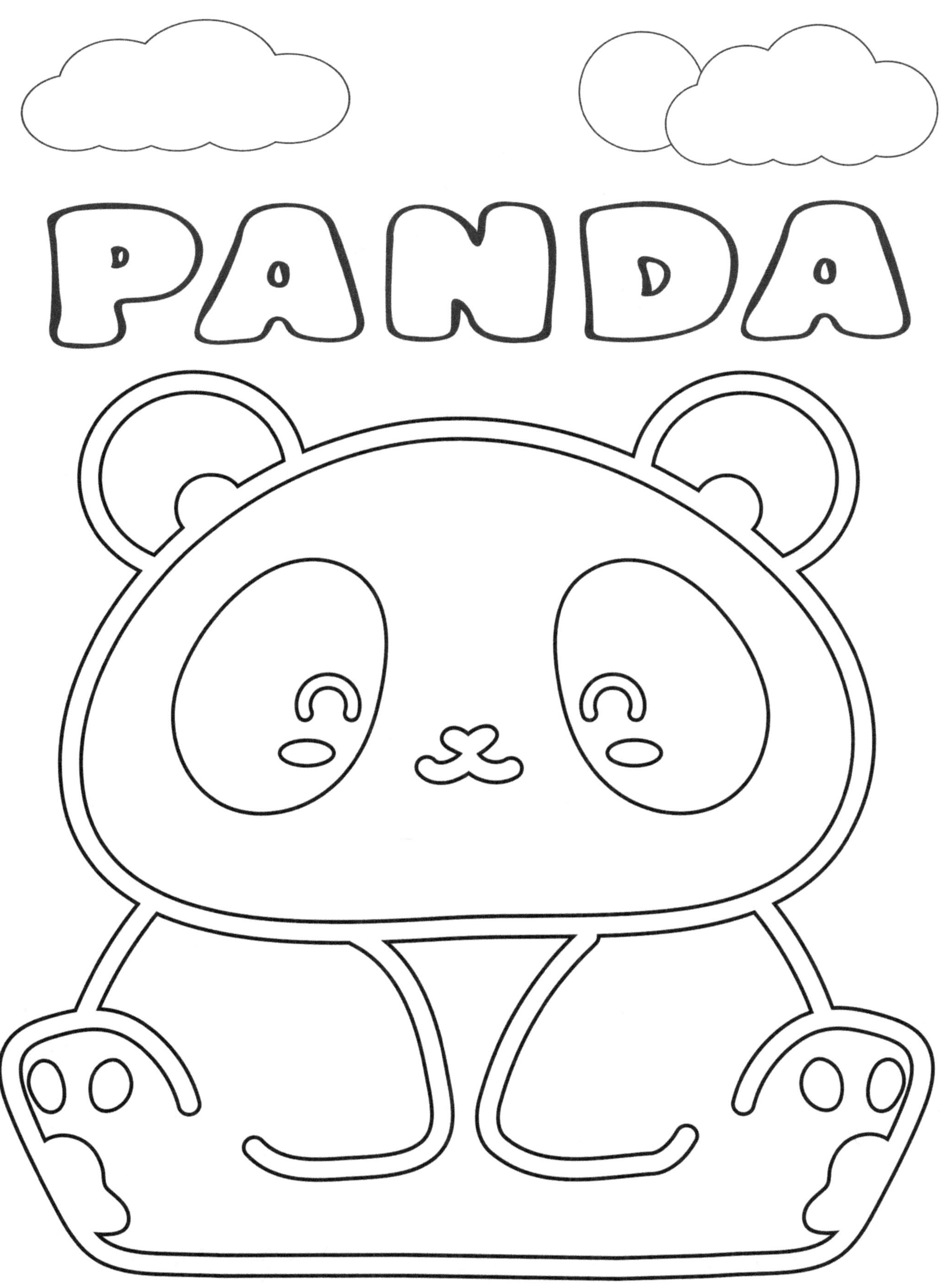

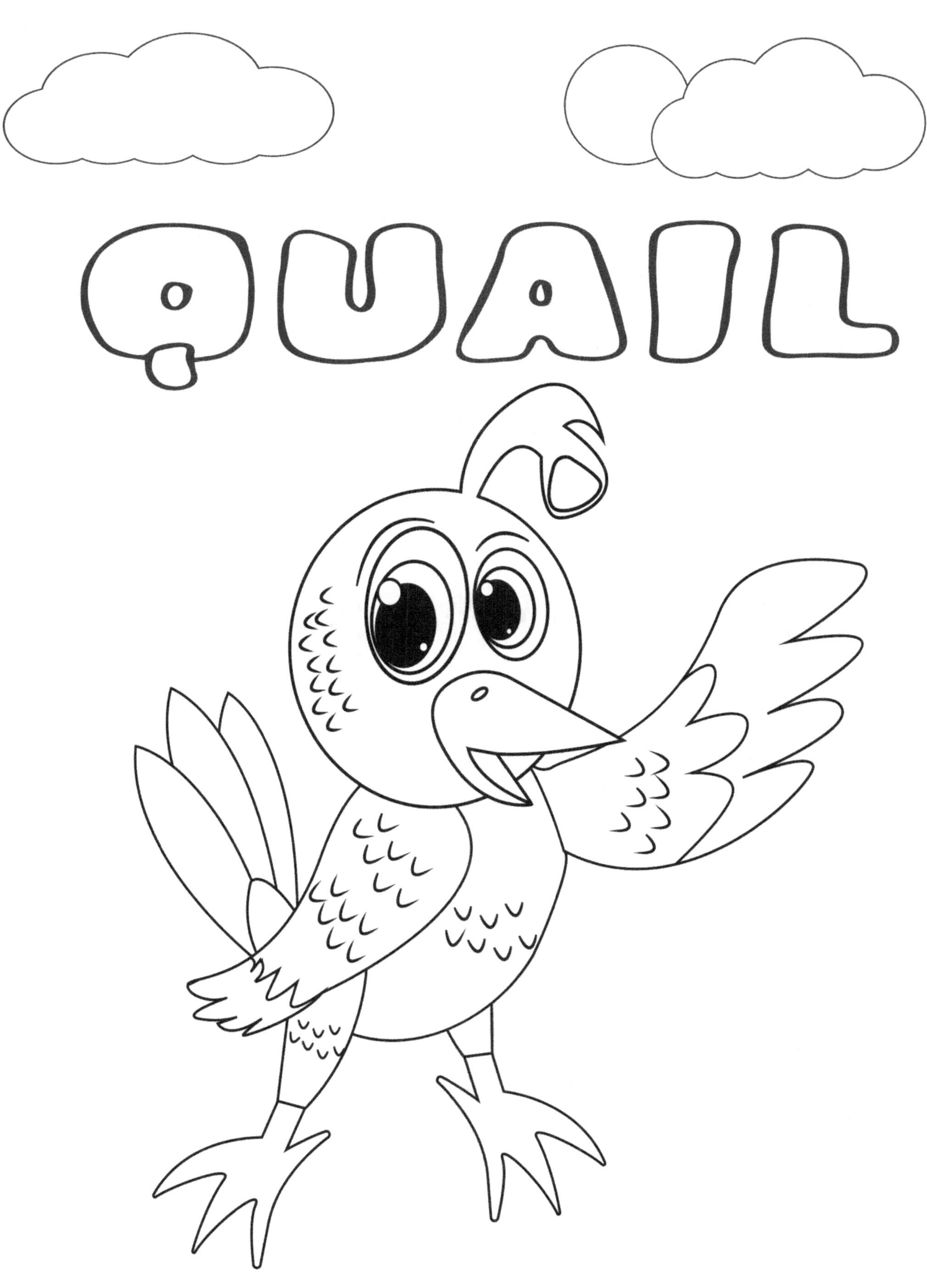

QUAIL

RABBIT

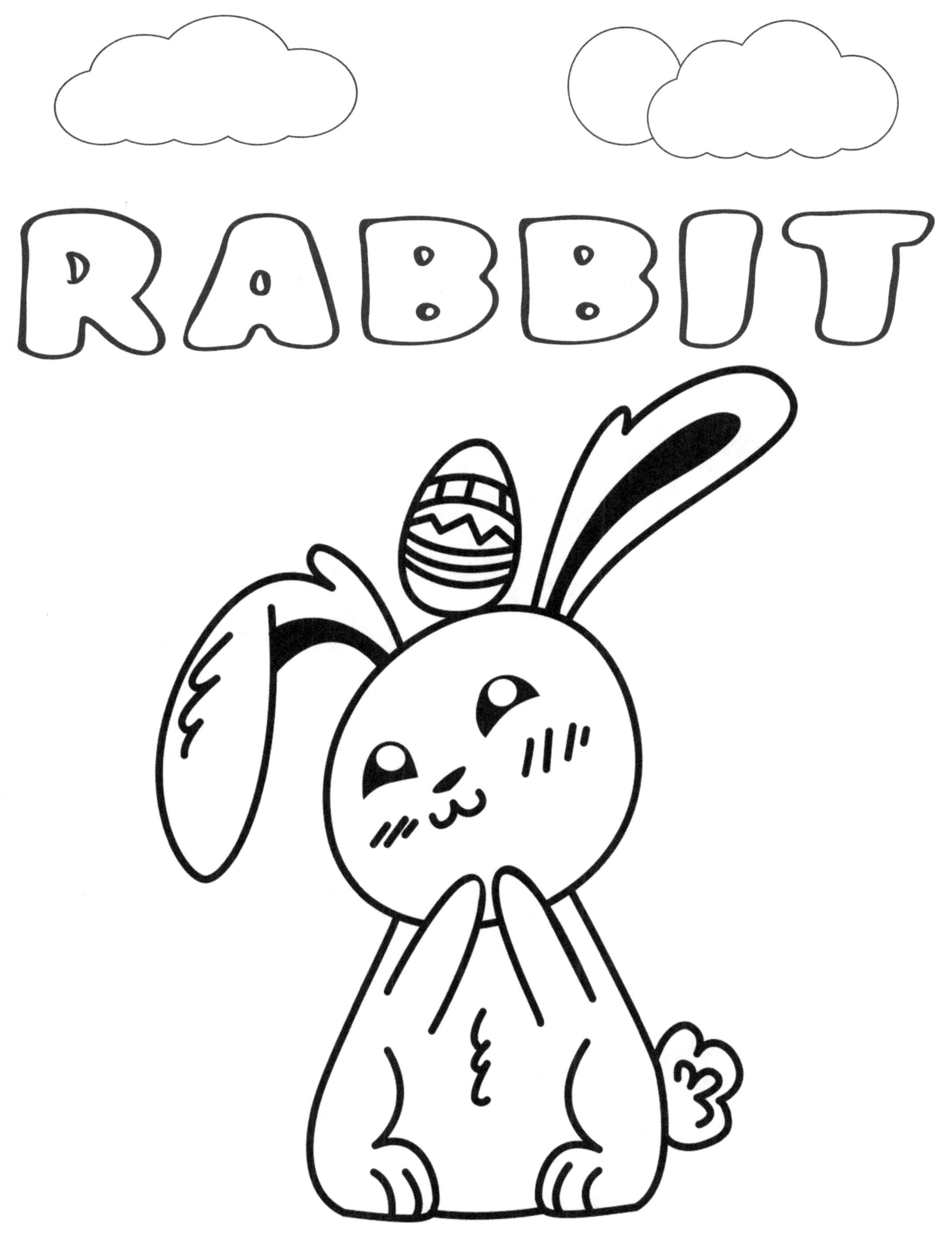

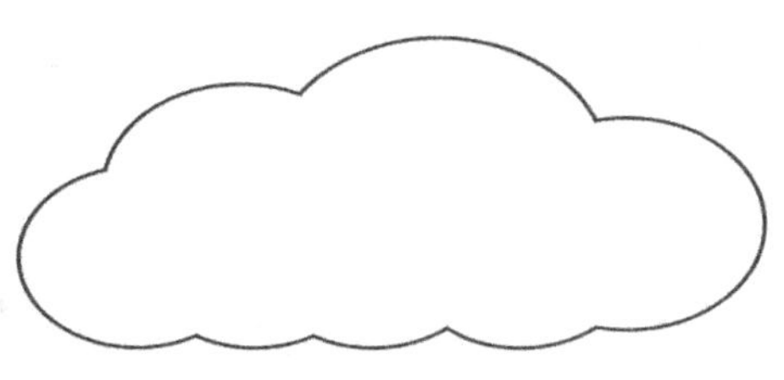
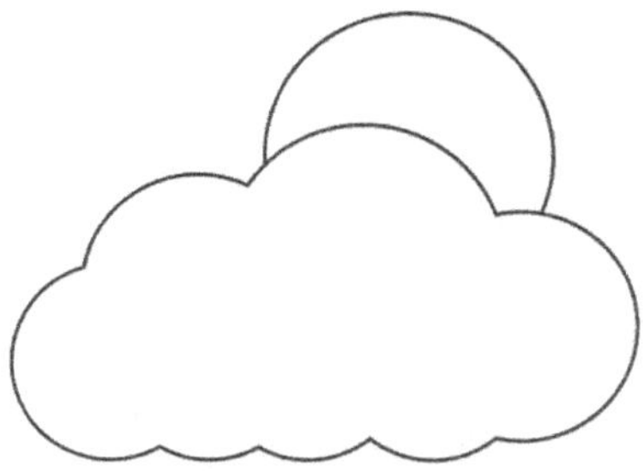

SNAKE

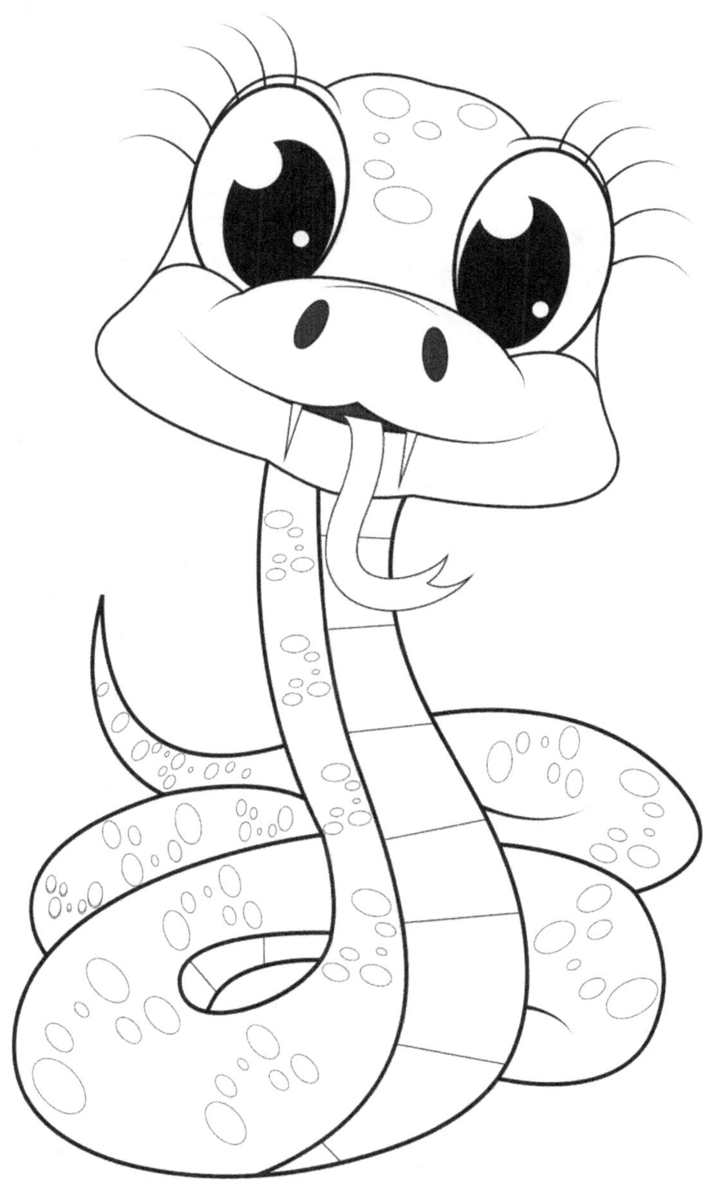

TIGER

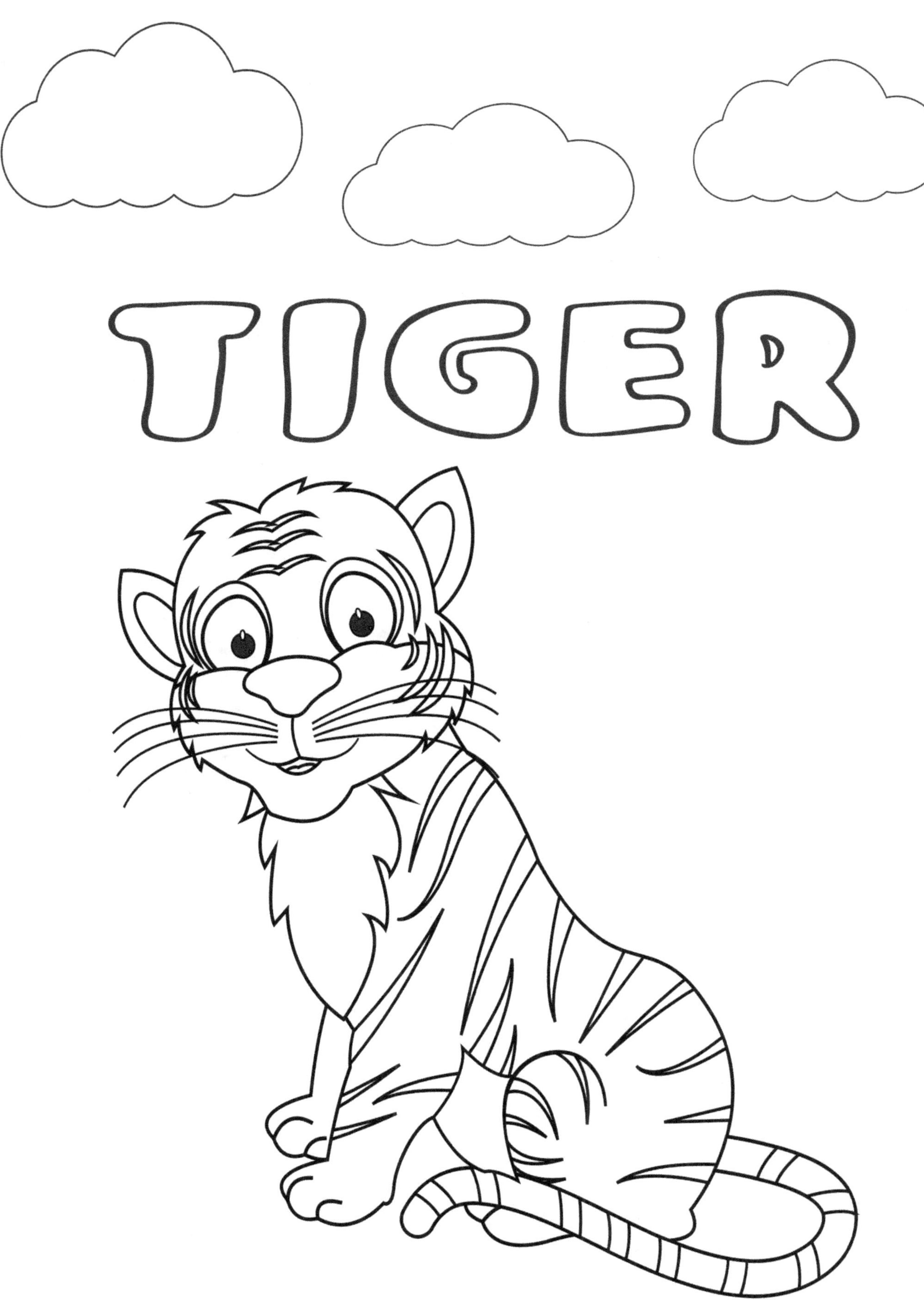

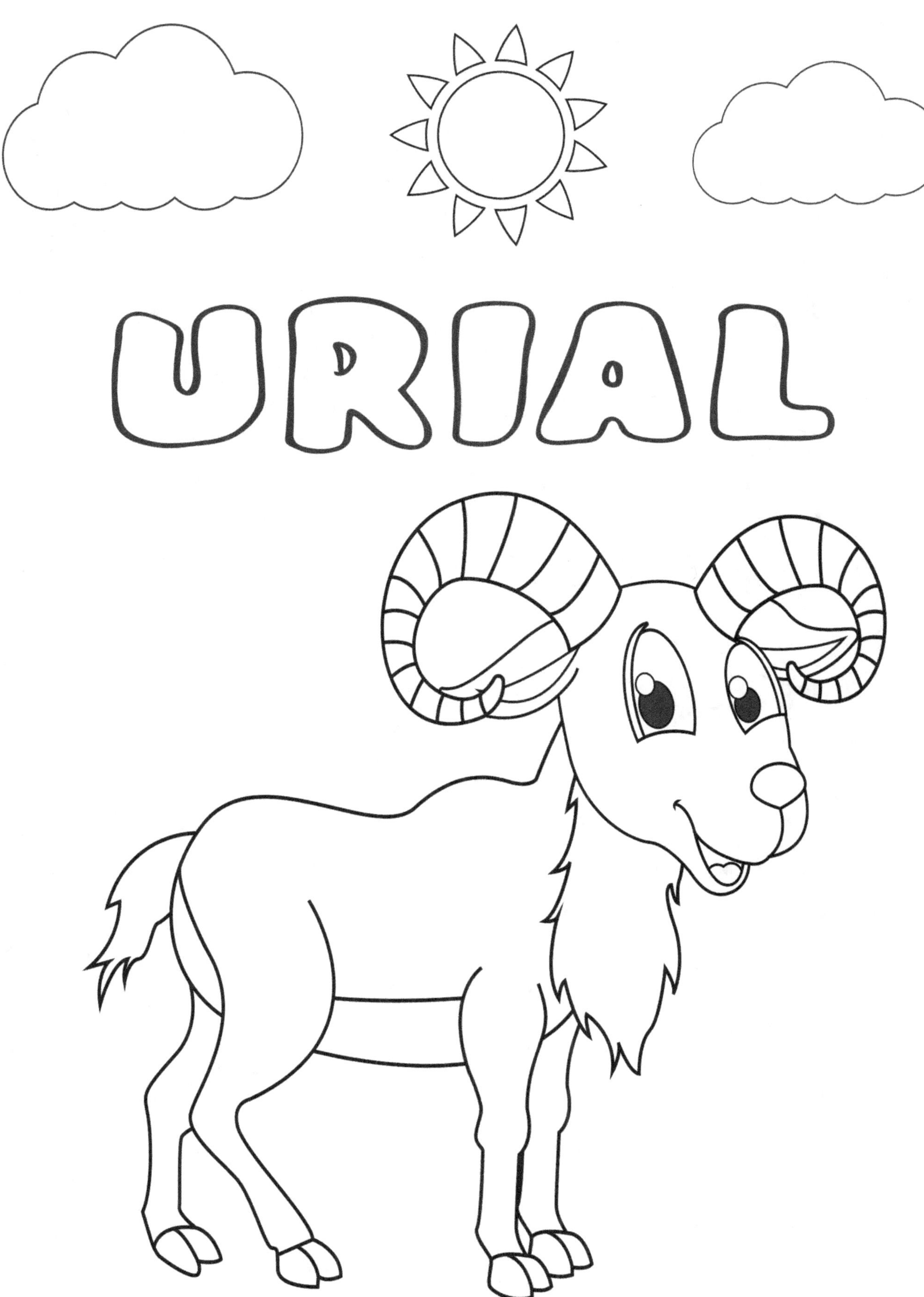
URIAL

VULTURE

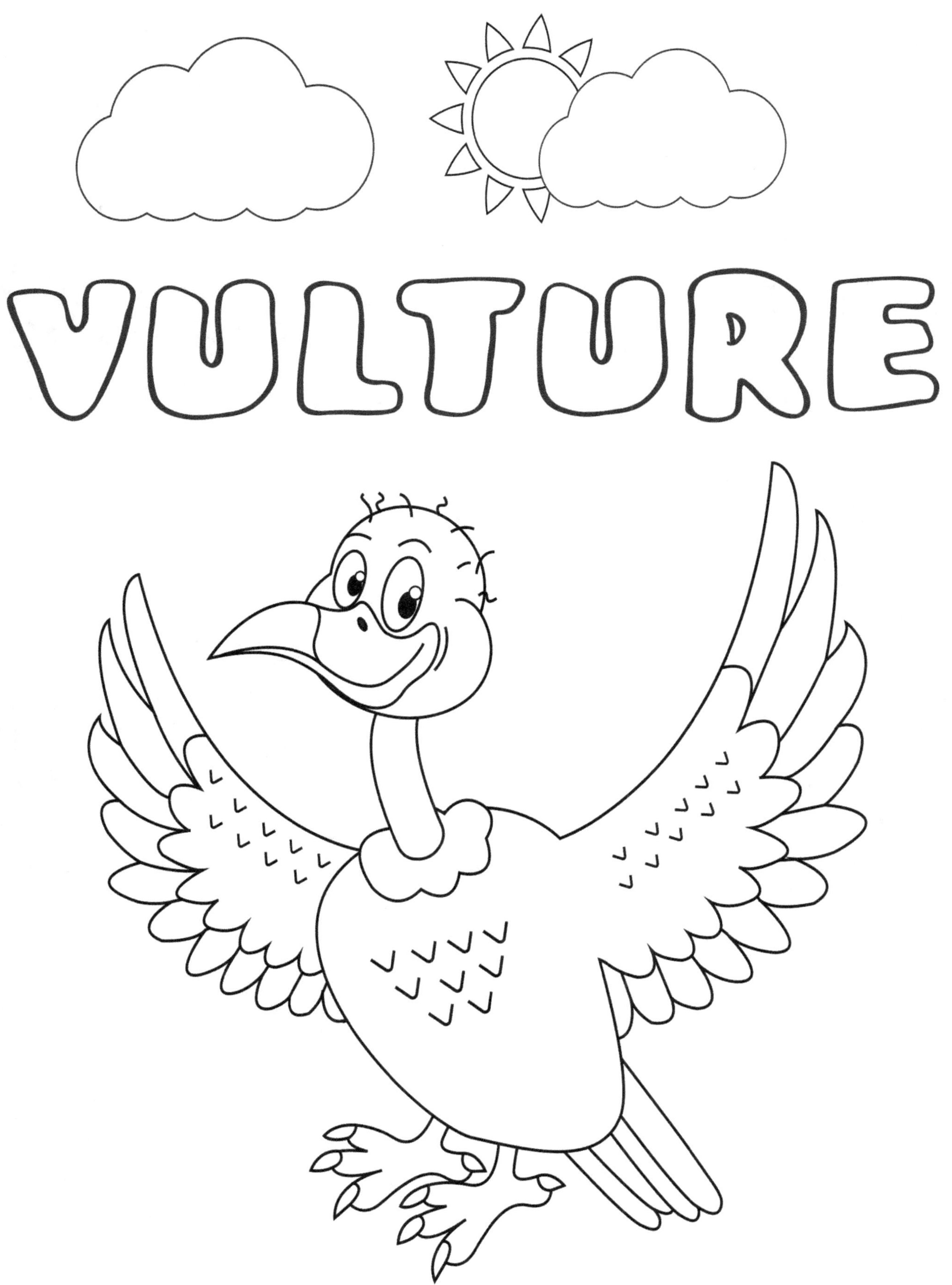

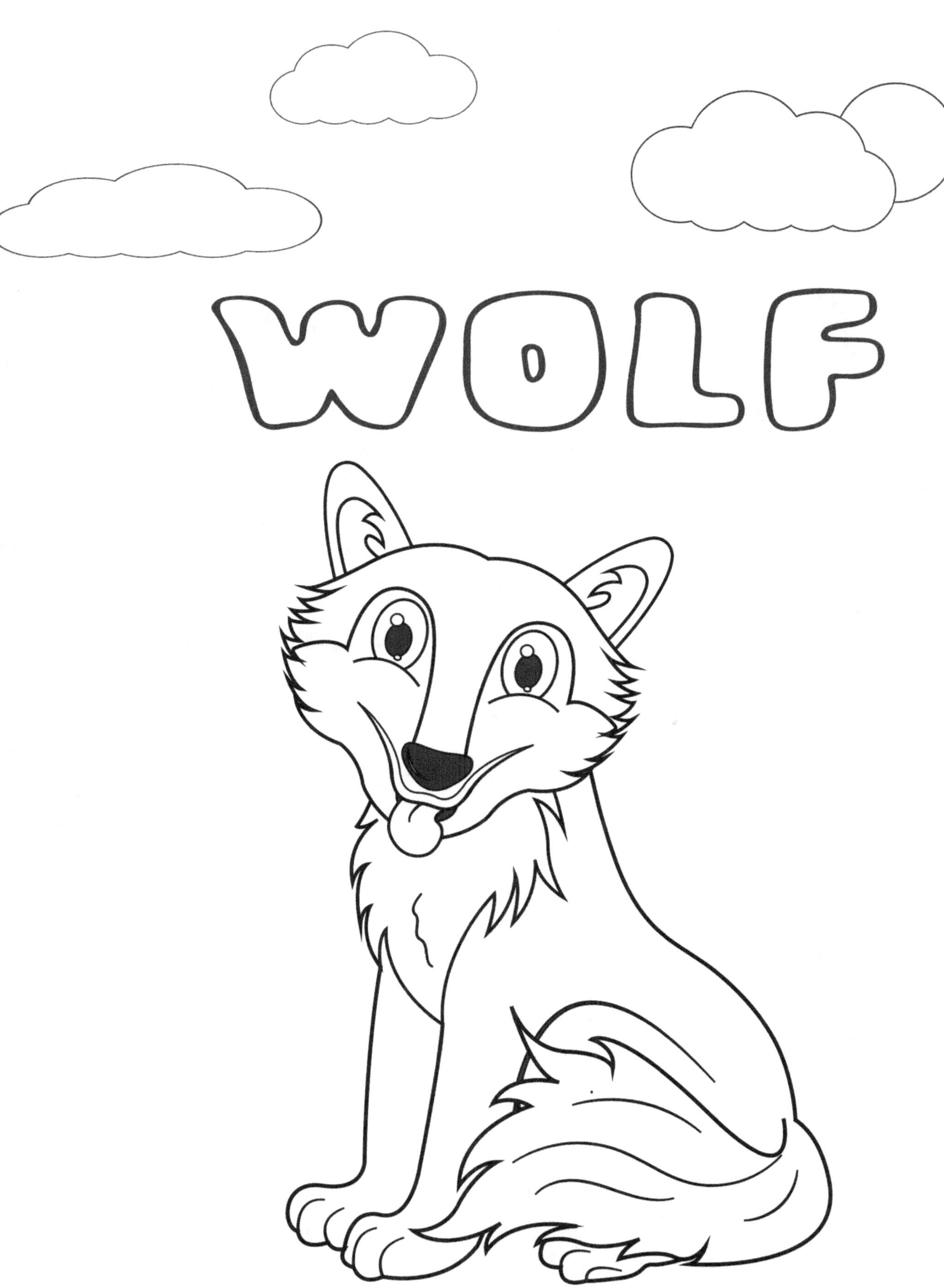
WOLF

XETRUS

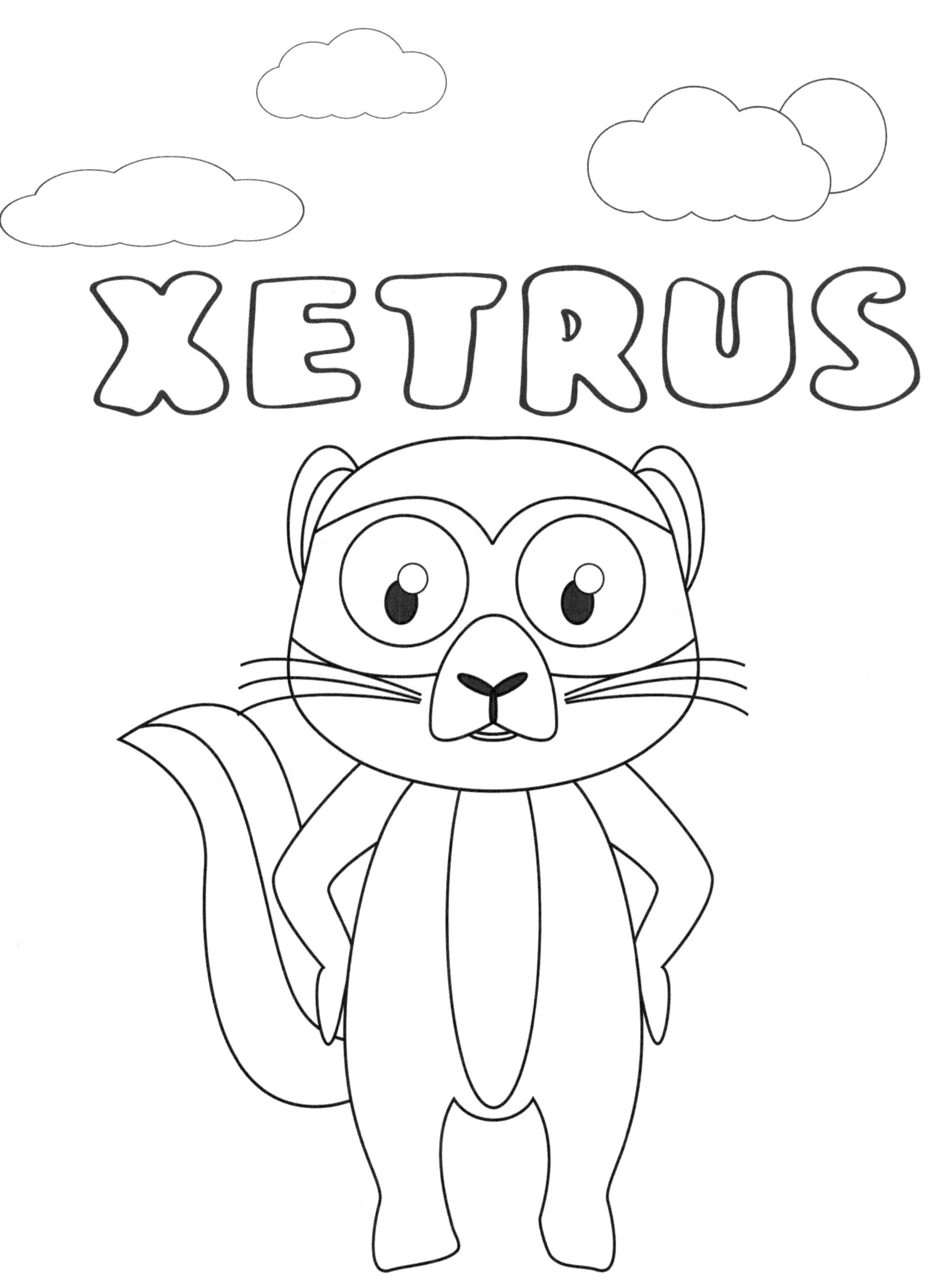

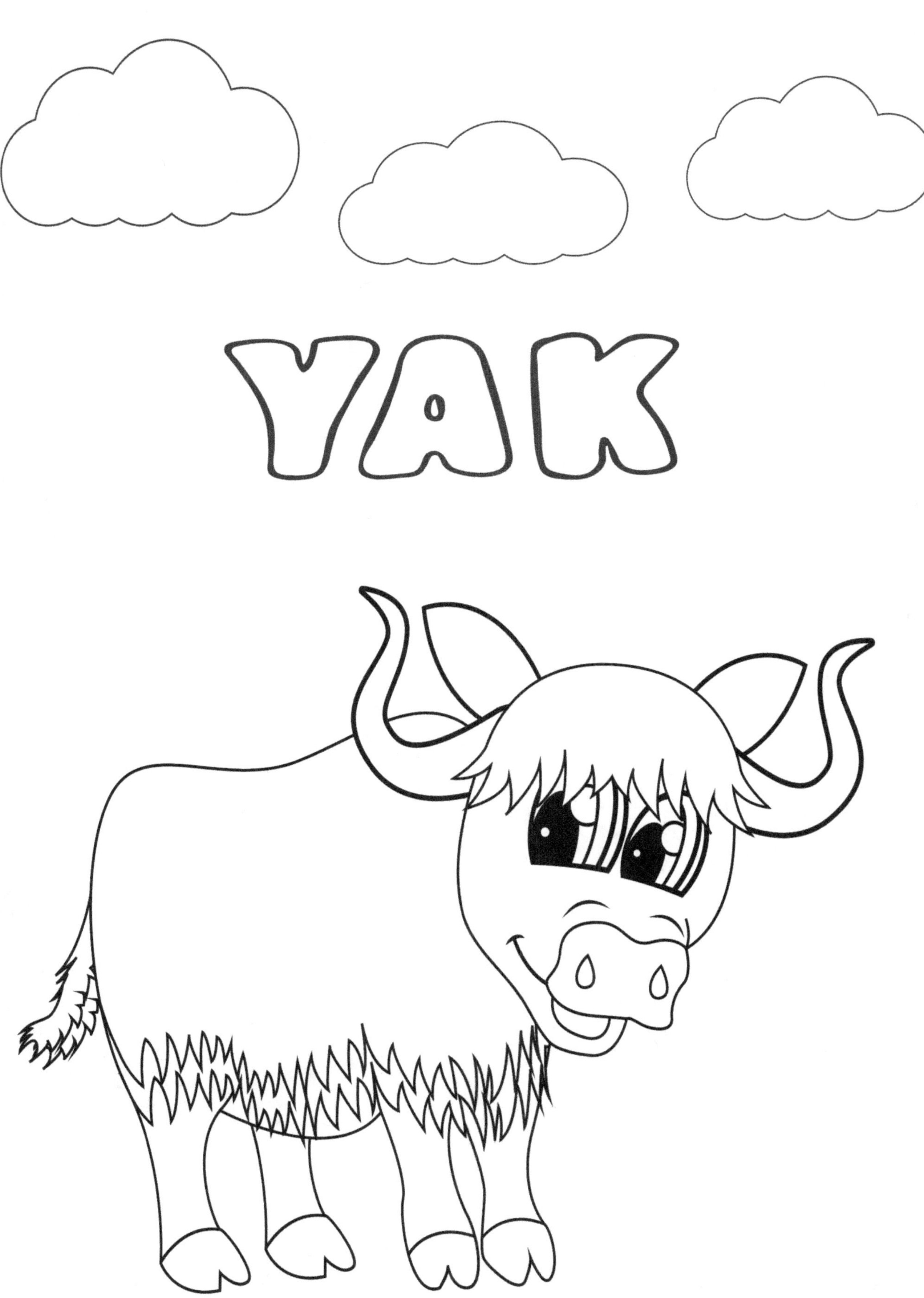

YAK

ZEBRA

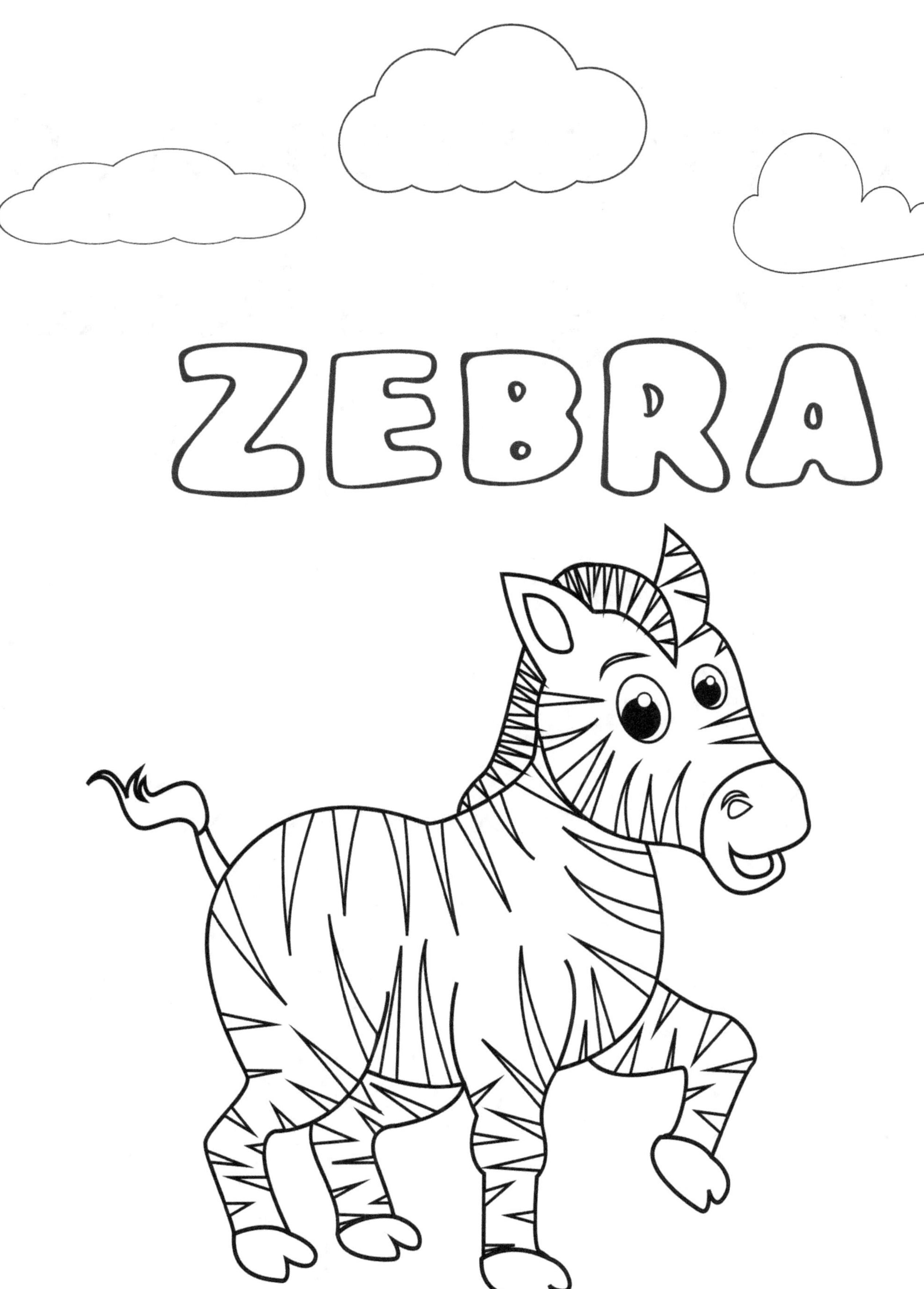

I hope you enjoyed coloring this book.